Calling **Dibs**, **Jinx**, **Shotgun**, and Other Things **No One** Knows the Rules To

D0992876

www.theresajulian.com
Email: NAAAHRules@gmail.com

This book is dedicated to all the kids who — like me — rarely got shotgun, never got the last slice of pizza, and barely had a chance to hold the remote.

Let's settle the score, shall we?

ISBN: 979-8-9852526-0-6
Copyright © 2021Meraki Books, LLC

Join our
JOKE CLUB!

To join, send an email to:

NAAAHRules@gmail.com

and receive:

- ■ 8 Hilarious Would You Rather questions
- ■ 8 You-Be-the-Judge Challenges
- ■ New **funny** surprises every month!

Then visit our website to learn about all of our books!

www.theresajulian.com

Table of Contents

Introduction

First, you're welcome.

We start with that because we know you'll thank us since this book will end arguments over the burning questions in life, such as who gets the last slice of pizza, who gets to hold the TV remote, and who's "it" when you and your buddy both call "not it" at the same time. This book lays out the rules for the everyday stuff no one knows the rules to in an attempt to restore peace in family rooms across the globe.

Not only does this book list the official rules for everything from frontsies to rock paper scissors to thumb wrestling, it also includes a challenge in each section. If you make your friend laugh during a You-Be-The-Judge challenge, you score a point. Whoever gets the most points is the

1

official Game Master Supreme and has bragging rights for an entire week.

You heard us: **an entire week**.

The rules for games like dibs, jinx, and shotgun vary from country to country, state to state, and school to school. So, if you're wondering who was bold enough to take the variations of all these games and establish one set of official rules, it would be us, the National Association of Absurdity and Hogwash **(NAAAH[1])**. If you have a beef with our interpretation of the rules, please call us at 1-800-THE-RULES. Even though we value your feedback and have a firm commitment to customer service, please know we won't pick up the phone or ever call back. Why? Because we used all of our brain power to write this book, we hired a really smart lady with a giant red pen to proofread it, and we borrowed money to publish it from a scary guy with a neon tan.

Then — and most importantly — we called dibs on these rules.

So, sorry dude, these rules are official. **We called it**.

---

[1] *If you're wondering how to pronounce* **NAAAH**, *it's like this: Should I decide the important things in life using research, key metrics, and fancy statistics?* **NAAAH**, *I'd rather use a made-up game that's based on sideways logic and has tons of gray area. It's just more fun.*

Rules to You-Be-the-Judge Challenges

After each topic in this book, there are three challenges. The challenges are meant to test your knowledge (and make you laugh)! To participate in the challenges:

1. Start with two players or two teams.
2. Player 1 reads a challenge out loud and answers the question. They have 30 seconds to explain their answer in the most hilarious way possible.
3. If Player 2 laughs within 30 seconds, Player 1 gets a point. If Player 2 is able to keep a straight face, they get a point.
4. The player with the most points at the end of the challenge, or set of challenges, is **Game Master Supreme** and has bragging rights for an entire week!

Warning: The scenarios in this book are solely for fun and games! Please do not attempt any of the crazy scenarios in this book at home or anywhere.

Calling Dibs

We begin with dibs because of its power and importance in shaping the world as we know it. It all started when the first caveman spotted a juicy wild boar and called dibs. Since then, dibs has morphed into a powerful force in the universe, deciding border disputes, ending wars, and creating dynasties.

In case you've been living under a rock, dibs is the act of claiming something by being the first to call it. Many people don't know this, but dibs played an important role in triggering the American Revolution. Contrary to popular belief, the Boston Tea Party was not about angry colonists protesting British rule. Turns out it was two dudes who called dibs on a tea bag at the same time. They fought over who had dibs, one thing led to another, and . . . you guessed it, over it all went into the harbor.

Now that you know the importance of dibs, turn the page and **get crackin'** on learning the rules!

The RULES!

Calling Dibs

1. **Visibility.** The thing you're calling dibs on must be real and in plain sight. No calling dibs on something that's buried at the bottom of the car trunk, a picture on a website, or a future thing, like the pan of fudge brownies your sister is going to bake.

2. **The first to say "dibs" wins.** If two people say the word at the same time, both must count to ten and whoever gets there first wins. If both reach ten at the same time, play a quick game of rock paper scissors (see page 24) to break the tie.

3. **Witness required.** No calling dibs when you're alone. Someone between the age of 4 and 104 must hear you say "dibs" and, if asked, will attest to it in a court of law.

4. **No dibs by proxy.** You have to be the one to call it. You can't send your little brother outside to call dibs on the best bat for the home run derby so you can lie on the couch watching the season finale of America's Got Talent.

5

5. **Dibs are not reversible.** If you call dibs on the big donut with chocolate sprinkles, and then get closer and realize it's crawling with ants and not sprinkles, sorry dude, it's yours.

6. **Dibs are nontransferable.** You can't gift them to a friend, frenemy, or the girl/boy you're trying to impress.

7. **Only trivial things can be dibbed.** You can call dibs on stuff like using the good video game controller but not things like a winning lottery ticket, someone's new bike, or the A your friend got in math.

8. **Like cheese, dibs expire.** If you call dibs on the window seat in the art room (because it's papier-mâché day and the room stinks), your dibs expire once art class ends. The next time you have art, the window seat is back up for grabs.

9. **Be a considerate dibber.** If you dib over aggressively, your friends may get steamed and not want to hang out with you anymore. If that happens, you'll be dibbing by yourself which, as stated in Rule #3, is against the rules—so be cool!

you be the JUDGE!

Calling Dibs

Challenge 1

You and your sister both want to borrow your cousin's cool new music T-shirt, and you both called dibs at the same time. However, you said the entire word, and she only said "ibs" to get it over with quicker. You don't think "ibs" should count because doing things halfway never counts, like crossing a river halfway and baking a cake halfway. However, she argues that it should count because you both ended at the same time.

Who gets to borrow the T-shirt?

Challenge 2

You called dibs on holding the TV remote and you won. However, once you touch the remote, you realize your brother spilled syrup on it, and then the dog licked it all over and buried it under the crumb-filled couch cushion. Your brother insists that you hold the remote because dibs are not reversible. You argue that you shouldn't have to hold it because it's hair-raisingly horrifying.

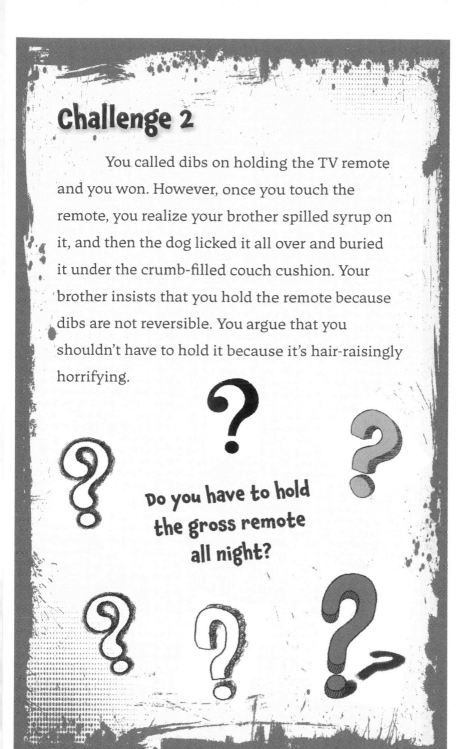

Do you have to hold the gross remote all night?

Challenge 3

This may be hard to believe, but both you and your friend are in need of a new kidney. When she gets a call that her new kidney is in, you jump up and call dibs. She argues that you can only call dibs on trivial things. You disagree, saying that a kidney only weighs ¼ of a pound, which makes it really quite trivial.

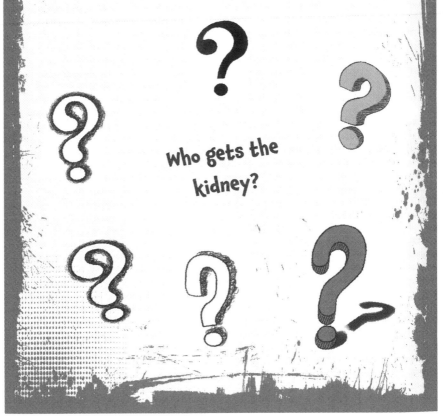

Who gets the kidney?

Not It

"Not it" is pretty much the opposite of dibs. Instead of calling something you want, it's calling something you don't want. Like when you're fishing with your uncle and he asks for a volunteer to put worms on the hooks, you can call "not it". All of the rules to dibs apply to "not it":

- You have to call it first.
- That call is not reversible, transferable, or proxyable and will eventually expire.
- Certain types of things don't apply to "not it." Don't get janky and try to call "not it" on homework or your turn to teach Grandma how to send an email. Someone's got to do it!

Calling Jinx

It's no coincidence that "jinx" and "stinks" rhyme because if you get jinxed, it totally stinks. Jinx is another iconic game which begins when two people say the same word at the same time, and then one, or both, call jinx. The penalty for getting jinxed is you have to buy the other person a soda, and you're not allowed to speak until you do. If you get jinxed in a place like the Sahara Desert or the Arctic Circle where there's no soda, you're doomed to a speechless day. Because of the stiff consequences, we at **NAAAH** suggest you learn the rules of jinx, especially if you plan on traveling to a remote location, aren't a fast thinker, or can't afford soda.

The RULES!

Calling Jinx

1.   **Calling jinx.** After two people speak the same word at the same time:

- The first to say "jinx" wins.
- The loser then owes the winner a soda and can't talk until the soda (or suitable substitute) is handed over.
- If the winner says the loser's name before the soda is given, the game ends and no soda is owed.

2.   **Saying jinx simultaneously.** If two people say the word at the same time, both must count to ten and whoever gets there first wins. If both reach ten at the same time, play a quick game of rock paper scissors (see page 24) to break the tie.

3.   **No soda.** If the loser can't find a soda or—let's face it—is too cheap or lazy to buy one, they can't talk until midnight when the game ends.

4. **Soda? Really?** Like dibs, jinx is an ancient game which evolved before the invention of Red Bull, flavored water, and Gatorade. Therefore, we at **NAAAH** are adding an updated twist. In addition to soda, you can give the winner any fun drink that doesn't come out of a faucet and the dentist would hate.

5. **Tricking *is* allowed.** If you ask someone a question such as "What day comes after Tuesday" they'll probably say "Wednesday." If you both say "Wednesday" at the same time, you can quickly call jinx and your friend (who may not be your friend for much longer) must endure the consequences.

6. **Sounds count.** During the no-talking period, the loser can't laugh, grumble, moan, or snicker. If the loser makes any type of mouth-related noise, they owe the winner a second soda. (The loser can cough or sneeze only if they're actually sick and can prove it with a doctor's note.)

7. **Coincidence must be verbal, not visual.** If you notice your friend is wearing an orange dress that's the exact shape and color of the safety cone she's standing next to, you can't call jinx because the coincidence is visual, not verbal.

8. **Writing is allowed, but not texting.** During the no-talking period, the loser can handwrite a message but can't text a message. We add this stipulation because writing is a lot of work and texting is easy, and no one said losing jinx would be easy!

Calling Jinx

Challenge 1

Your friend won jinx, and you can't find soda anywhere. You're afraid you're facing a speechless day until your friend calls you Teddy, which was your childhood nickname. You claim (on paper) that you should be able to talk because she said your name. She argues that Teddy doesn't count because it's not your real name. Fake things never count, like fake ID, veggie stix, and astrology.

Should nicknames count as saying the other person's name?

Challenge 2

You lost at jinx, can't find a soda, and are resigned to keeping your mouth zipped for the rest of the day. However, your friend starts cracking jokes, making faces, and speaking in silly accents, and you can't stop laughing. It gets to the point where you owe him a truckload of soda. You claim (on paper) that he's unfairly causing you to laugh. You say he should stop cracking jokes and instead sit quietly, stare at the blank wall, or chew on his shoelaces.

Is it fair if one person makes the other laugh just so they'll get more soda?

Challenge 3

You're having lunch with a friend at a decent restaurant. You bend down to tie your shoe and you both notice that your plaid socks match the wallpaper at the restaurant. Your friend is flabbergasted at the coincidence and calls jinx. You claim she can't jinx you because a socks-wallpaper match is visual, not verbal. She argues that the coincidence was so bizarre, it just has to count.

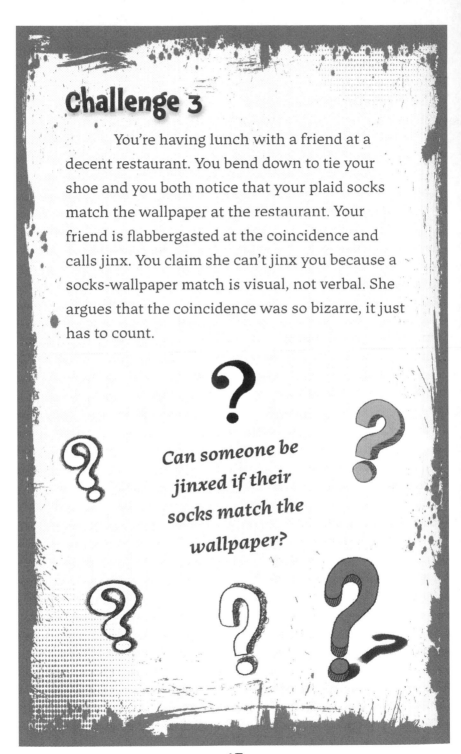

Can someone be jinxed if their socks match the wallpaper?

Calling Shotgun

Ah, the seat of power!

Think Rome during the Roman Empire, that giant red chair in Buckingham Palace, and the front passenger seat in a minivan—which happens to be the prize in shotgun. Scoring the front passenger seat is big because it ensures you have the car ride's best view, direct access to the driver, and possibly control over the music—all pretty solid perks. To win shotgun, simply be the first to shout "shotgun" once the car is in sight. Then settle into the front passenger seat, get your co-pilot hat on, and start planning your dominion over the peons jammed into the back seat.

The RULES!

Calling Shotgun

1. **First to call it.** If you're the first to call "shotgun," the front passenger seat is yours. If two or more say "shotgun" at the same time, the driver decides who sits in the seat.

2. **Car must be in sight.** You can only call shotgun when you're walking to the car and the car is in plain sight. No calling it before you see the car, after you're already in the car, or when you're still in the house—screaming out the window.

3. **Caller must be ready.** The shotgunner must be dressed, with shoes on, and bags in hand. They can't run out half dressed, call shotgun, then go back inside and finish getting ready. Though that would be hysterical, it's not fair.

4. **No texting shotgun.** We can't believe we have to say this, but no texting shotgun. Some things just don't transfer into electronic messaging, like hugging a parent, petting a puppy, or calling shotgun. Plus, shouting shotgun in front of the house and carrying on like a monkey in a zoo is more fun than the tiny ding of a text message.

5.   **Like death, shotgun is a one-way trip.** For the return trip, the game resets and the privilege is back up for grabs.

6.   **Vomit avoidance.** If a passenger is turning green and looks like they may vomit, they automatically get shotgun so they can toss their cookies out the window. Even though this is rule #6, it supersedes all other rules because, yeah, vomit is that gross.

7.   **Physical domination.** If no one's around to hear you call shotgun, climb on in because the seat is yours. If the door is locked, put your hand on the front passenger door and get in when the driver unlocks it.

8.   **Call backseats next.** After shotgun is decided, passengers can call other seats in the car by saying things like "back right window" or "not middle seat."

9.   **Moms, grandmas, and the driver's significant other.** These passengers always get shotgun even if they don't call it. At first, this rule may seem unfair. Why do mom-like people always get the front? **Because we said so!** Now stop asking questions, get your butt in the backseat, and be thankful you have a car to ride in.

NOTE: Small children are not allowed to sit in the front seat of a car, no matter how good they are at calling shotgun. Rules vary by state, but children are only permitted to sit in the front if they weigh a specific amount or are a certain height. We joke about a lot of things in this book, but we're not joking about this!

you be the
JUDGE!

Calling Shotgun

Challenge 1

You and three friends call an Uber. When the car arrives, the driver is eating a sardine sandwich and slurping a florescent green smoothie. One friend calls "reverse shotgun" which means she's *not* sitting in the front. You argue that there's no such thing as reverse shotgun because lots of things in life can't be reversed, like getting your appendix out, letting one rip in a quiet classroom, and un-eating a cake.

? *Should reverse shotgun be allowed?* **?**

Challenge 2

Your family's going to Aunt Ida's birthday party. Your brother runs out of the house without a shirt or coat on in the middle of winter just to be the first to call shotgun. You claim he shouldn't get shotgun because he wasn't actually ready. He says he was ready; he'd been planning on going to the party shirtless because it's a cool look.

Should someone get shotgun even though you know they weren't ready?

Challenge 3

Your family is taking a car ride around a lake where there are always lots of cyclists, farm vehicles, and cute ducks crossing the road. Even though your sister won shotgun, you claim that she shouldn't sit in the front because you're much better at looking out for those things than she is. The last time she rode shotgun around the lake, your family car nearly clipped a biker and flattened a family of ducks.

Should someone who won shotgun fairly get it, even though they're not shotgun-worthy?

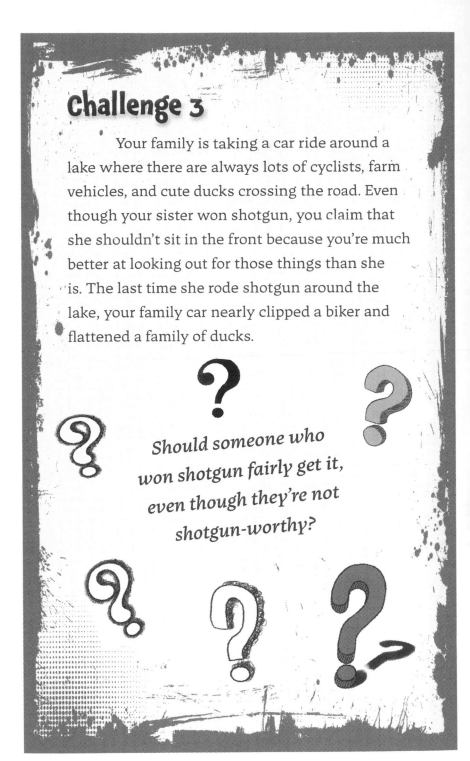

Rock Paper Scissors

If you paid attention in history class, you know the Hundred Years' War was long, confusing, and lasted more than 100 years. What you may not know is that after five generations of fighting, the exhausted leaders ended the war with a quick game of rock paper scissors[2]. They wrapped it up like this because rock paper scissors, also called ro-shambo can shut down a dispute in about 12 seconds. The game is played when two opponents form either rock, paper, or scissors with their hands. Different shapes beat other shapes (as explained on the next page), and the first person to win two throws is the victor. In addition to being quick, rock paper scissors doesn't require any equipment—besides, of course, two hands and a teeny drop of brain power.

[2] The part about how the Hundred Years' War ended isn't exactly true, but we think it should be because it's so much easier to understand. No offense Hundred Years' War, but you really were a complicated train wreck.

The RULES!

Rock Paper Scissors

1. **How to play.** Both players pound a fist into their open palm three times, saying "rock, paper, scissors" and then form one of the following shapes while saying "shoot":

- Rock – a closed fist
- Paper – an open hand
- Scissors – the index and middle fingers forming a V

2. **What beats what.**

- Rock crushes scissors
- Paper covers rock
- Scissors cut paper

If you both throw the same shape, just re-shoot.

3. **Best two out of three.** A game consists of three rounds of "shooting" and the best of two out of three wins. A one-and-done round is permitted if you're so busy you can't spare the extra seven seconds to play the full game and both players agree ahead of time.

4. **Paper beats rock?** A common question is on what planet can paper beat rock? First, paper *covers* rock; it doesn't beat rock in a knock-down-drag-out fight because, well, that would be ludicrous. Second, if you're using a silly hand game like rock paper scissors to decide something important, you shouldn't even be asking this question. You abandoned logic long ago.

5. **Shape must be recognizable.** If no one's around to hear you call shotgun, climb on in because the seat is yours. If the door is locked, put your hand on the front passenger door and get in when the driver unlocks it.

6. **Last minute change.** Changing your shape after you see what your opponent has thrown means you've cheated, and "cheated" rhymes with "deleted," which is what you are if you pull that. Game over, you lose.

7. **Create your own version.** You can recreate a new version of the game with your own words, like sock scraper wizard, if both players agree to the words and shapes ahead of time. Our only caveats: all words must be PG, and tongue twisters aren't allowed since some of our readers have claimed that after playing with tongue twisters for too long, they can't talk for days.

you be the JUDGE!

Rock Paper Scissors

Challenge 1

You and your sister play rock paper scissors to determine who gets to pick the family dessert. On the deciding round, you throw paper and she throws what looks like paper, but her index and middle finger are split and she claims it's scissors. You remind her that she must throw a clearly formed shape. She says she slammed her hand in her locker and now all of her fingers seem to have minds of their own. She insists that her misshapen muddle of fingers are scissors, even though they don't look anything like it.

Who gets to pick the dessert?

Challenge 2

The toilet is clogged, and your parent says either you or your brother must get the plunger and clear the clog. You play rock paper scissors to decide who is stuck with the nasty job. Once you're on the deciding round, you shoot but your brother doesn't. He stands paralyzed with fear that the dreaded job will be his. He says he regrets leaving the fate of unclogging a smelly toilet to the weird triangular logic of rock paper scissors. He hasn't lost but hasn't won either, and he is too afraid to shoot again.

Who should plunge the toilet?

Challenge 3

You're playing rock paper scissors with a kid who loves to smash things: pumpkins, balloons, watermelons, etc. You just know he'll throw rock both times, so you throw paper twice and win. He can't figure out how you won so quickly and accuses you of pulling some kind of weird Jedi mind trick. You say you used your brain, not a trick. A mind trick is when you levitate an ice cream out of someone's hand, eat it, and then convince them it was their idea to give it to you.

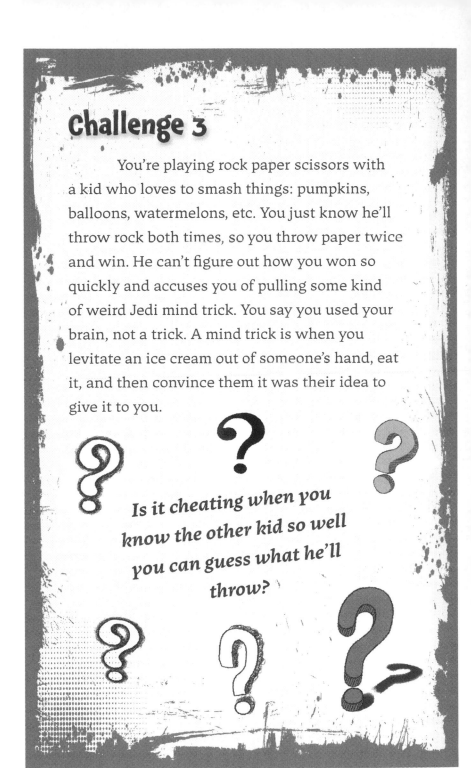

Is it cheating when you know the other kid so well you can guess what he'll throw?

Frontsies and Backsies

"Frontsies" and **"backsies"** sound like silly kid words, but letting someone get in line before or after you is really quite serious. Picture this: you're standing in line at a buffet, absolutely starving, and you notice there's only one shrimp and two chicken wings left. Your friend saunters up and asks for frontsies. You know she's a fellow shrimp/chicken wing lover, and you're so hungry you're ready to chew your feet off. In a case like this, do you give her frontsies? Backsies? See what we mean? Frontsies/backsies isn't child's play; it's a solemn legal transaction and it behooves you to learn the rules.

The RULES!

Frontsies & Backsies

1. **Frontsies are allowed.** Most people on planet Earth agree that when you're standing in line, the square of air in front of you is yours. You have the explicit legal right to do whatever you want with it: swing your arms in it, dance in it, or give it to a friend. The people in line behind you aren't allowed to complain, but sadly, they sometimes do. If this unfortunate situation occurs, be sure to quote to them these **official** rules. If they still aren't convinced, tell them to call us at **1-800-THE-RULES.** We'll straighten them out.

2. **Direct backsies aren't allowed** since you're, in effect, giving away the frontsies of the person behind you, and that's not yours to give away. It would be like giving away someone else's football skills or their cool new haircut. Impossible. However, we at **NAAAH** have figured out a workaround, which is called switcheroo frontsies (see below).

3. **Switcheroo frontsies.** This is when you offer frontsies to a friend, and then your friend offers frontsies to you. After the switcheroo, you're in front of your friend and you have, in effect, given them backsies, albeit in a perfectly legal way.

4. **Backsies has two meanings.** This confuses a lot of people. Backsies is letting someone stand in line behind you, and it also means undoing a swap, such as trading your bag of carrots for someone's chips and then yelling "no backsies." We want to make it clear that we're talking about the first type of backsies—who gets to stand in line behind you—not what happens to your gross bag of carrots.

5. **Multiple frontsies.** We get this question all the time: Can you let in more than one person? Okay, now you're pushing it. In most cases we say no; however, multiple frontsies is allowed under special circumstances. For example, it's allowed if you're standing in line for the bathroom and you have more than one friend who needs to puke, pee badly, or wash their hands because they just cleaned the frog tank in the science room and their hands are covered in frog schmear.

6. **Cuts.** Cuts is just a cooler name for frontsies/backsies but follows the same rules. (BTW, "cuts" is always plural, such as "Can I have cuts?")

7. **Saving places.** This is sticky because saving places depends on the situation.[3] What if you're in line for a cool rock concert where the singer pulls people onto the stage? Under those circumstances, it's not fair. So, our answer is . . . it depends. Some questions just don't have a clear answer: How long is a piece of string? What's really inside a Twinkie? Can you actually count to infinity plus one? We rest our case.

[3] This is the rule for saving places in line. For rules on saving seats, see page 36.

you be the JUDGE!

Frontsies and Backsies

Challenge 1

Ah, modern technology! It often complicates simple situations. Let's say you've been standing in a take-out line for an hour. You finally get to the front of the line when some guy breezes in front of you and grabs his Philly cheese steaks to go. You ask why he's cutting, and he says he used the restaurant's online app to order and now, voilà, his food is ready. He quickly pays and leaves with a sarcastic "Sorry, sucker!"

Is it fair to use technology to get frontsies?

Challenge 2

For years you've been #64 on the soccer team. Then a girl who always argues with you joins the team and picks #63. Now when the coach lines you up in number order, she's ahead of you. You tell her she needs to change her number because you never gave her frontsies. She says frontsies don't count in sports. When you're running a cross country race and want to pass someone, do you ask for frontsies? When you're running the bases in softball, do you ask the first baseman if you can pass?

Do frontsies and backsies count in sports?

Challenge 3

You're in line at the movies, and your friend comes late, so you give her switcheroo frontsies. The lady behind you has never heard of switcheroo frontsies and doesn't want to let your friend stand in front of her. The lady can't comprehend the circular logic and says your friend is really taking backsies, which is expressly prohibited. You ask her to call 1-800-THE-RULES for clarification but, well, there's no answer. The lady demands that your friend go to the back of the line with the other late people.

Since switcheroo frontsies is based on circular logic, should it be allowed?

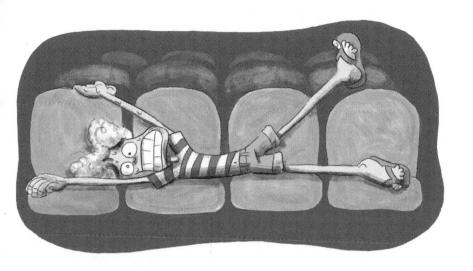

Saving Seats

Picture this: you walk into a concert that has open seating. You get there early but can't nab great seats because some kid is trying to save the entire front row. He doesn't have enough jackets to drape across all the seats, so he's lying across four seats and trying to save the rest with socks, shoes, a dirty tissue, and a banana peel. He probably ran out of stuff to put down because on the last seat is a wilting pile of banana strings (those sticky threads inside of a banana). Is that fair? Can you save a seat with banana strings? And how many seats can one person save? The questions loom large. It's important to learn the rules so your next open seating event doesn't turn into The Hunger Games.

The RULES!

Saving Seats

1. **Number of seats.** Can one person save ten seats? 20 seats? More? We adhere to the 2:1 rule which means one person can save up to two seats, in addition to his own. Here is our rationale:

- Save one? Fine. It's probably for your goof-off friend who's always late.
- Save two? Okay, we know everyone has a second friend who always pees at the last minute.
- Save more? No. If you have more knucklehead friends than these two, you need to make new friends, preferably ones who are on time.

2. **Time limit of saved seats.** What if you hold seats and the people never show up? Or they breeze in after the show starts, step on everyone's feet and trip over stuff as they stumble down the aisle? We say you can hold a seat until five minutes before the show starts. After that, the seats are fair game.

3. What saves a seat?

- Preferably outer clothing such as a jacket or sweater. (Definitely no inner clothing, and by "inner," you know what we mean.)
- Something from the event like a program or brochure (if you go to events that are fancy enough to have these things).
- Other things are acceptable only if they're clean (no muddy shoes) and are bigger than a Rubik's cube. Don't try to save a seat with something tiny like an eraser or Lego man.

4. Can you steal a saved seat?

If rules 1 through 3 are followed, no, you cannot. If you do, you probably won't get arrested, but good luck sitting next to the steaming-mad person you stole it from. (And if you leave at intermission, check the seat for a wad of gum or spilled soda before you sit back down.)

5. You can save ground space.

If you're at a beach or outdoor concert, the 2:1 rule doesn't apply because it's too hard to calculate. In terms of ground space, you can save as much ground as your blanket or towel can cover.

6. You can save air space.

If you're at an event where everyone's standing, you can save air space by waving your arms around in the air you want to save. Our guess is no one will want to stand next to you anyway.

you be the JUDGE!

Saving Seats

Challenge 1

You get a good seat at a movie you're really psyched about. You're watching the trailers and notice some girl is trying to save a whole block of seats but doesn't have enough stuff to put on the seats. She asks to borrow your jacket, sweater, shoes, and whatever you'll give up so she can save this block. You hesitate, first because she's clearly a seat cheat who's breaking the 2:1 rule, and second, you don't want to strip down to save seats for someone else's friends.

Should you loan clothes to some random seat cheat so she can sit with her friends?

Challenge 2

You thought you'd seen it all. Clearly, you haven't because you're at an outdoor concert and notice two kids who forgot blankets and are trying to save ground space by "starfishing" which is laying on the ground with legs and arms spread like a starfish. They're violating rule #5 which says you can save ground space but, at the same time, complying with the implied logic behind rule #6, which is act crazy so people just let you have the space.

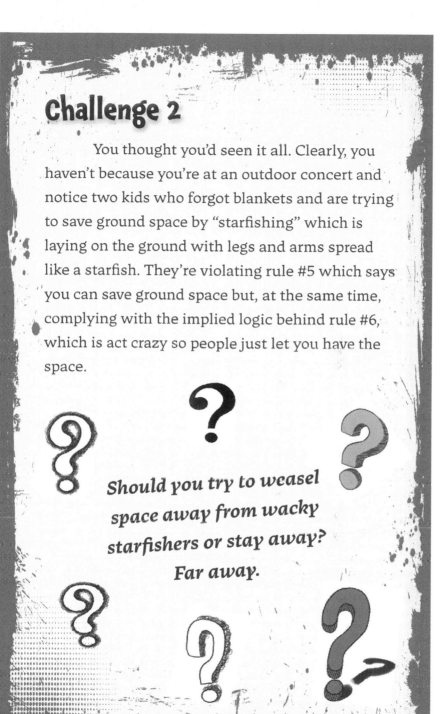

Should you try to weasel space away from wacky starfishers or stay away? Far away.

Challenge 3

Your friend saved you a front row seat at a comedy show you've been dying to see. When you get there, he points to the saved seat. It's covered in brown goop which could be dirt, brownie crumbs, melted brown crayons or . . . (You stop there. You don't want to keep guessing.) You ask why he saved you such a crappy (no pun intended) seat and he says he didn't notice and you should be happy he nabbed it. Now you either have to sit on the dirty seat or take a seat in the back.

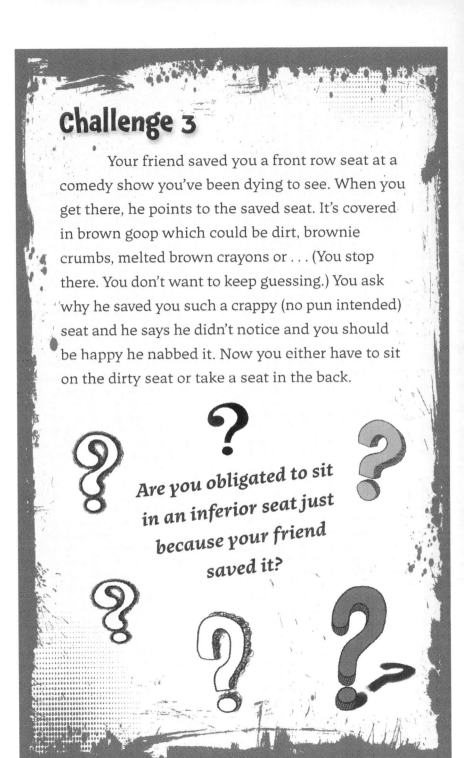

Are you obligated to sit in an inferior seat just because your friend saved it?

High Fiving and Fist Bumping

Have you ever held up your hand for a high five and instead of a firm slap gotten back a light tap? Or a missed five? A slipped five? A four? A pat on the head? Or you hold your fist up for a bump and someone leaves you hanging? We at **NAAAH** think all of these are unacceptable. Since high fives and fist bumps are important ways of saying "hello," "I agree," and "great job," we think you need to learn how to execute them properly. For a solid five or perfect bump, you need practice, skill, timing, agility, and confidence so you can avoid this type of wing nuttery:

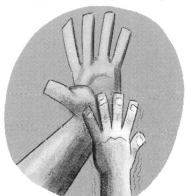

"The Slipped Five"

"The Missed Five"

"The Bad Bump"

The RULES!

High Fiving and Fist Bumping

1. **When and where.** Can you fist bump in the hall? *Yes*. High five at a football game? *Yes*. High five at a funeral? *No*. At an expensive wedding? *No*. Opera? *No*. Civil War re-enactment? *Nah*, a quick nod is probably better. When you're at an expensive or solemn event or dressed in fancy clothes, show some class and refrain from all bumping and slapping.

2. **Use good technique.** Don't raise your hand too early or too late. If you raise it too early in a high five, pretend you meant to and turn it into a friendly wave. If you raise it too early in a fist bump that's not returned, bring your hand up and smooth your hair as if you just got a cool new haircut. For high fives, connect with your friend's hand in a simple, quick, vertical slap. No squeezing, grasping, twisting or lingering. Fist bumping is a quick tap, straight on, knuckles to knuckles.

3. **Usage Limit.** High fiving or fist bumping more than once an hour is unacceptable. Slapping and bumping are like writing in all caps: great when used occasionally, but if you use it too often, it's like **SCREAMING**.

4. **Wi-fives.** Wi-fives (when hands are raised but not slapped) are acceptable during a global pandemic, on a FaceTime call, and if your friend is an extreme germophobe. Wi-fives are different from missed fives because they're intentional, not a clumsy mistake.

5. **Choosing how to connect.** This decision is up to the initiator. Instead of the high five, it's okay to low five, fist bump, forearm bump, hip bump, nod, bow, salute, and on occasion, curtsy. The rule is return what's given.

6. **Is handshaking still a thing?** Dads shake hands. Moms air kiss. Anyone born after the cell phone was invented usually high five, fist bump, or give a chill "what's up?" nod.

7. **Must agree.** If you don't agree with what your friend wants to high five about, you don't have to return it. Like if she says "Let's run into the haunted house, turn on the lights, and scream 'come and get us'," and you prefer to remain alive for the rest of the night, don't high five back.

you be the JUDGE!

High Fiving and Fist Bumping

Challenge 1

You're in the cafeteria and a friend approaches —someone who's really nice, but totally awkward. She raises her hand and raise yours to return the five, but then she switches to a low five. You move your hand down, and she raises hers, fist-bump style. You raise your hand too, but she winds up fist bumping your forearm and somehow shoulder bumping you at the same time. You wind up doing a kind of wiggle dance in front of everyone. You tell her next time she has to go through with the first thing she starts so you don't look like pea-brains in front of the whole school.

Are you allowed to restrict your friend's high fives if she can't make up her mind?

Challenge 2

Tomorrow's T-shirt day at school. Your buddy says, "Let's both wear our baseball T-shirts," and holds up his hand for a fist bump. You bump him back and later realize he said "Neanderthal," not "baseball." You both had weird matching Neanderthal shirts in fourth grade, and those are the ones he wants to wear. Once you realize this, you tell him you don't want to. He says you have to because you bumped on it. You say you're retracting your bump. He says there's no such thing as retracting and you have to wear the Neanderthal shirt.

Do you have to go through with something just because you fist bumped on it?

Challenge 3

Your crush is heading down the hall wearing his cool denim jacket. He's smiling and his hair seems to be blowing in the breeze, even though you're indoors and there is no breeze. He puts up his fist in a weird, tilted way and your mind goes blank. He pushes the fist toward you, and you figure it must be a pretend microphone. You grab his hand and start belting out your favorite karaoke song only to realize he was trying to fist bump.

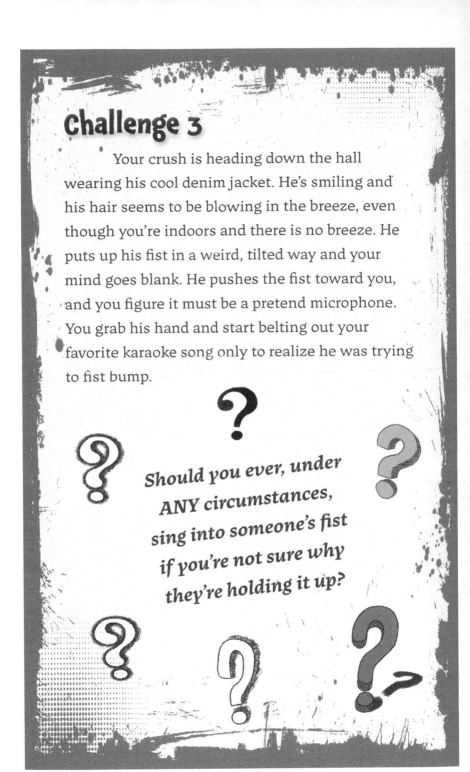

Should you ever, under ANY circumstances, sing into someone's fist if you're not sure why they're holding it up?

Paper Football

American football is a tough, blood-

and-guts game played on the gridiron. Paper football is a
flicking and sliding game played on your mom's coffee table.
With paper football, there's no shoving, grunting, or tackling.
There's no painting your face or dumping Gatorade over your
friend's head. In fact, there's not even a foot—or a ball. So, if
you want to have fun but also want to keep your teeth, play
paper football. It's safer.

The RULES!

Paper Football

1. **Make a paper football.** (The instructions are on page 54.) And yes, the football must be paper. No flinging Doritos, slices of pie, or other triangular things.

2. **Going first.** After you make the football, put a mark on one side. One player calls the mark, the other calls blank, and then flip the football to see who goes first.

3. **Player one pushes the football** so that it slides from his side of the table to his opponent's side. If the football hangs off the edge without falling off, the player scored a touchdown (six points). If it doesn't make it to the edge or falls off the table, it's the other person's turn. Notes:

- When we say slide, we mean *slide*. No bouncing, throwing, whipping or catapulting. Keep it together, this is a real sport!
- If there's a question as to whether or not the football is over the edge, take a book (not this book because it's too valuable) and use it to swipe the edge of the table. If the football moves, it's over the edge.

- Only friction (the actual invisible force that slows things down in the universe) can stop the football. There's no blowing on it, waving your hands, or dancing in front of it, hoping your body breeze will stop it.

4. **Kicking a field goal.** When the offensive player scores a touchdown, he gets to "kick" a field goal:

- The defensive player creates a goal post by putting his thumbs together and pointing his index fingers in the air.
- The offensive player balances the paper triangle on a tip and flicks it through the goal post with the thumb and index finger of his other hand. If the ball makes it through, the offense scores one point, and his turn ends.

5. **If the football lands on the ground.** The player who didn't send it to the ground "kicks off" and then takes his turn. To kick off, lay the football in the palm of one hand and smack it with the other hand so the football flies up. Wherever the football lands is where play begins again.

6. **Winning.** The game ends when one of these things happens:

- You've agreed to play to a certain point value (such as 10) and one player reaches that number.
- Your teacher storms toward you with her hair on fire and yells that study hall is for studying.
- The football has fallen on the floor so many times it's now covered in dog drool, greasy fingerprints, and cookie

you be the JUDGE!

Paper Football

Challenge 1

Your parent just polished the game table and it's now covered with a thick, shiny coat of Lemon Pledge. Now the table is more like a Slip 'N' Slide than a game board. (But, bright side, it does have a delightful lemony scent.) Your buddy insists that you play on this table because it's the one you've always played on. You agree, but halfway through the game you realize there's no way you can keep from overshooting on this slippery, slithery nightmare.

Should you end the game in a draw and move to a grease-free table, or are you obligated to see a game through on the table you started with?

Challenge 2

You're playing paper football with your little sister who won't stop sliding the football across the table with her nose. She claims the rules don't prohibit nose sliding. Even though you protest, she won't stop because she's actually doing really well. However, the football is now so covered in nose goo you no longer want to touch it.

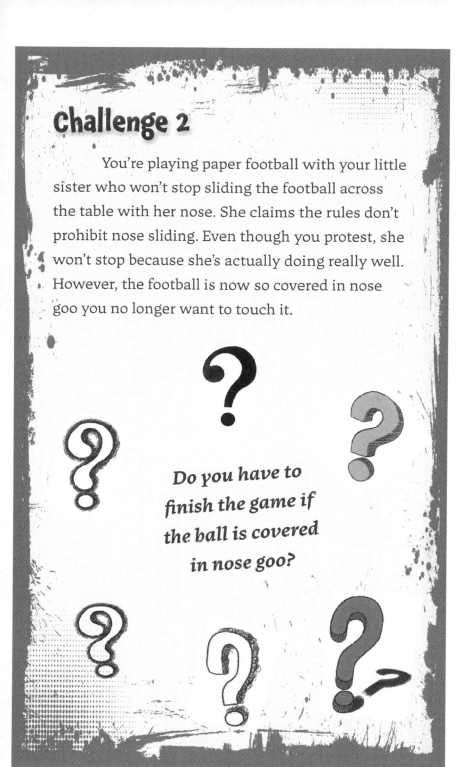

Do you have to finish the game if the ball is covered in nose goo?

Challenge 3

You're on the last play of a big game and it's come down to one final field goal. You balance the football on the tip of your finger, lean down, and gaze across the table with an intimidating look. Your friend raises his fingers in a goal post position and shoots back an icy stare. Game on! You flick the football, and it whizzes across the table, sails through the goal post, and hits your buddy square in the forehead. He yells that he's hurt and the field goal should be a do-over. He argues that in all sports, play is stopped when someone is hurt.

?

Do you re-shoot a field goal if your friend got knocked on the head, or do you tell him this is only paper football and he needs to suck it up?

How to Make a Paper Football

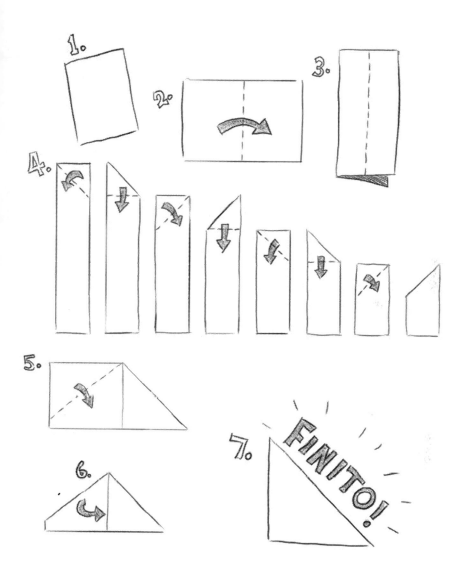

Opposite Day

See you later. Goodbye!

When we say "goodbye" we mean "hello," which is what you do on Opposite Day. You say the opposite of what you mean or do the opposite of what you normally do, like wear your shoes on your head. Eat cake for breakfast. Walk backwards. Tutor your friends in math, but instead of teaching them how to be *good* at it, teach them how to be *bad* at it. The possibilities are endless.

Then, when you finish reading this, tell your friends how bad this book is. We hate selling books, and we want to make sure everyone knows this one **stinks**.

The RULES!

Opposite Day

1. **When opposite day starts** is a mind bender. If you say "it's Opposite Day," does that mean it's not Opposite Day? Technically, it'd be a normal day because you mean the reverse of what you're saying. But, if you say it's a normal day, how would anyone know it's Opposite Day? After debating this for weeks, the geniuses at **NAAAH** decided Opposite Day starts immediately after you proclaim "it's Opposite Day". So, here goes: *we at **NAAAH** declare today is Opposite Day*. Now please send us angry letters about when Opposite Day starts.

2. **Must be a complete reversal.** Opposite means as different as possible. Therefore, on Opposite Day you can't do or say things that are just a little different. They have to be completely opposite like wearing gloves on your feet or brushing your teeth with candy. It's Opposite Day, not Sort-of-Different Day, or Kinda-Twisted Day, or I-Need-an-Excuse-to-Wear-My-Fluffy-New-Fur-Coat-in-the-Middle-of-Summer Day.

3. **Any day can be opposite day.** If you search "When is Opposite Day," Google will tell you it's January 25th. Or August 17th. Or when a black cat walks past a broken mirror. Since Google can't make up its mind, and because it's too much fun to be only once a year, we decided Opposite Day is any day you declare it. Did you hear that Google? Back off! ~~NAAAH~~ sets the rules on stuff like this!

4. **Can be retroactive.** We've all been there: something stupid escapes from your mouth, and you wish you could pull it back and stuff it back down your throat. Well, now you can! If you say something dumb, instead of following it up with a lame "I'm only kidding," try proclaiming it Opposite Day. Of course you didn't really mean to say that your friend's singing sounds like he has pickles up his nose, you just wanted a smooth way to announce that it's Opposite Day.

5. **Use opposite day to accomplish a goal.** Let's say you've been dying to tell your friend that his gym clothes smell like potatoes, but you don't want to hurt his feelings. Instead, you can proclaim it Opposite Day and then tell him that his clothes smell like potatoes. Or soup. Or potato soup. He'll think you meant the opposite, but then he'll probably give his clothes a good sniff and realize...yeah.

6. **Can't be too extreme.** You can use Opposite Day to accomplish well-meaning goals, but you can't be too crazy and insult everyone in your family, neighborhood, and school. If your friend has a pimple that's big enough to be seen from space, keep your mouth shut. That's not a problem Opposite Day can solve.

you be the JUDGE!

Opposite Day

Challenge 1

You find yourself face-to-face with two angry muggers. You feel helpless because they're twice your size and their fists are ready. But you're a resourceful kid. You tell them it's Opposite Day and instead of taking your money, they need to give *you* money. They refuse, but you don't let up. You hammer them with Opposite Day rules until they exchange confused looks and start digging in their pockets for money.

Is it fair to trick muggers into thinking it's Opposite Day so they give you money?

Challenge 2

Your parents hand you a long list of chores you don't want to do. You tell them it's Opposite Day and you'll take over the parenting so they can get the chores done. They agree and hand you the bill for the car payment and mortgage, which you need to pay today. Just to be sure they're living up to Opposite Day, they ask you to buy food and make dinner. They point you toward the kitchen.

Since your parents really played you, do you follow through with your Opposite Day claim, or do you wiggle out of it like a scared little weasel?

Challenge 3

You approach your friend with a hat on each foot and your shirt on backwards and tell him it's Opposite Day. He claims it wasn't Opposite Day until *after* you said it and asks why you're dressed like that. You insist that it was Opposite Day as soon as you finished saying it was. He says you should have mentioned Opposite Day and *then* put the hats and shirt on. Now he won't join in because you didn't do things in the right order. You're left standing in the school hallway with hats on your feet and your shirt on backwards.

Should you have said it was Opposite Day and then put on the clothes?

Would you Rather

Would you rather have a giant rubbery tongue or feet that never stop growing? Would you rather sweat blue slime or maple syrup from your forehead? In the game Would You Rather, you answer questions like these and hope your response makes your friend laugh. The problem is you're usually given two equally bad choices, like choosing between eating eyeballs or brains. Or you're given two equally good choices, like having glow-in-the-dark skin or cool electrified hair. Tough, right? Technically, it doesn't matter which you pick, it only matters if you make your friend laugh. Or smile. Or crack up so hard the noodle soup he's eating spurts out of his nose.

The RULES!

Would You Rather

1. To play.

- Start with two players or two teams.
- Player 1 reads a Would You Rather question aloud, answers it, and has 30 seconds to explain why she picked that answer in the most hilarious way possible.
- If Player 2 laughs, or even cracks a smile, Player 1 gets a point. If Player 2 remains stone-faced, she gets a point.
- Then it's Player 2's turn to read a question.
- The game ends when you've reached a point value you've agreed to (such as 10), or your friend's laughing so hard she fell off her chair and can't keep going.

2. Making your friend laugh. You can use
silly faces, goofy voices, pretend slipping and tripping, and whatever other nonsense it takes to make your buddy crack.

3. **Don't complain.** If you don't like either choice, too bad. Like the guy at the mall who thought juggling chainsaws was a good idea, Would You Rather is based on mostly bad choices—just be glad they're not real!

4. **Answer can't be "neither."** That's too easy and usually not funny. Man up, boys and girls, and take a side!

5. **Answer can't be "both."** Let's say you get a question like "Would you rather have your face on a cereal box or be a trapeze artist?" and you really want both. You can't pick a combo answer like you want to be a box of cereal with tiny arms and legs so you can do fancy trapeze stunts. Though a cereal box on a trapeze is funny, it's not allowed.

you be the JUDGE!

Would you Rather

Challenge 1

You ask your friend if he'd rather have fingers made out of hot dogs or a head made out of Jell-O. He picks Jell-O, then closes his eyes, swings his head, and keeps chanting "Jell-O" in a deep, crackly voice. He never explains why he wants a Jell-O head, he just keeps repeating the word and moving his body in weird ways. When he gets on the floor and starts wiggling like a Jell-O blob, you laugh. He claims he won because you laughed. You say he didn't win because he never explained his answer.

Can you win by making your friend laugh without saying why you picked your choice?

Challenge 2

You're going on and on about why you'd like to have super smelly breath, and your friend is trying not to laugh. You can tell she's about to, but she's holding back with all of her might and winds up making a weird creaking noise, like how the stairs sound when you're sneaking around in the middle of the night with the last piece of cake. She insists that the bizarre noise wasn't a laugh, but you know it was a tiny chuckle.

Does a weird creaking noise count as a laugh?

Challenge 3

Your friend is explaining why he'd like a giant purple hook growing out of his head, but he's not doing a good job. His explanation is a great big nothing burger, filled with lots of "ums" and "uhs." Since he's new to the game, you give him suggestions like he could use the hook to hang a bag of Halloween candy on. He could swing from trees like Tarzan. He could style his hair around it and hide the fact that he really only has B+ hair. Eventually, you wind up making yourself laugh.

Does your friend get a point if you make yourself laugh?

Odds and Evens

Did you know there's a one in 1,000,000 chance you'll get hit by a meteorite? A one in 5,000,000 chance you'll die in a tornado? A one in 14,000,000,000,000 chance you'd even be born? [4] If you're reading this, you were obviously born and, therefore are pretty darn lucky! If you want to keep your lucky streak going, play odds and evens because your chance of winning is a whopping 50 percent. Odds and evens is a game in which two people put out an odd or even number of fingers to help decide something, such as who goes first or who gets the good chair (the one that doesn't smell like old pennies).

Oh, and by the way, there was a one in 11,762 chance you'd find this book, buy it, and read this page. So, wait. First you were born and then **THIS**? You should definitely play the lottery.

[4] Don't question these statistics. They were found on the Internet, which is definitely always right.

The RULES!

Odds and Evens

1. To play.

- Start with two players.
- One player picks odds and the other picks evens.
- Players stand face-to-face, with one fist behind their backs and the other in front of them.
- Both players say "One, two, three . . . shoot," and then put out any number of fingers on their front hand.
- Add the number of fingers shown on both players' hands. If the total is an odd number, the player who guessed odds wins. If the total is even, the player who guessed evens wins.

2. You must "shoot" straight. Hold your hands out in front of you and keep both feet on the floor. No spinning, no over the head moves, and definitely no fancy pivots. This is a time-honored game, not Dancing with the Stars.

3. **Zeros are allowed.** This means you can put out a fist with no fingers extended. We allow this because we love zeros. Computer code is made up of zeros and ones, and without computer code there'd be no smart phones, internet, or any way to order those cool 3D moon lamps with two-day shipping.

4. **No fractions.** This seems ludicrous but needs to be said. There's no putting out two and a half fingers (one folded down to the knuckle) because fractions aren't whole numbers and, therefore, aren't odd or even. And don't get us started on decimals, improper fractions, and common denominators because the only common denominator here is *stop asking questions like this!*

5. **Shoot with only one hand.** If both players use both hands, the numbers get high, and some kids wind up taking out a calculator. At that point, STOP, because then it's no longer a fun hand game, it's homework. There's a thin line between fun and homework, and we don't want to cross that line.

you be the JUDGE!

Odds and Evens

Challenge 1

There's an ape with a hockey stick walking down your street. You and your friend freak because the ape is heading toward the house of a lady who's hard of hearing and is always losing her glasses. You're afraid she won't realize the creature is an ape and invite it in for some of her famous strudel. You play a quick game of odds and evens to see who'll warn the lady and who'll distract the ape. You're so nervous, your arm does an unwieldy side swipe when you shoot. Even though you won, your friend says you lost because you didn't shoot straight.

If someone is nervous about an ape with a hockey stick, are they allowed to wriggle as they shoot?

Challenge 2

You and two friends are taking a tour of a sausage factory. You're goofing around and tossing each other a plastic meatball you bought in the gift shop. The meatball falls into the sausage batter, so you play odds and evens to determine who will tell the tour guide. You pick evens, one friend picks odds, and the other picks a number divisible by three. The total winds up being nine, so your friends win and you lose. You argue that the friend who picked "divisible by three" had a better a chance of winning, but your buddies say it's too late, you lost.

Who has to tell the tour guide there's a meatball in the sausage batter?

72

Challenge 3

You throw a zero and your friend says zeros don't count, even though they do. She then pummels you with "zero" questions: Can you ride in a car with zero gas? Hear zero knocks on a door? Live with zero food? If you were in zero gravity, you'd float around forever, and if you screamed and threw up, the vomit would float back in, and you'd choke and die a horrible death. At that point, your head is spinning, and you can't stop thinking about vomit floating **into** your mouth. You give in and agree she won, even though she didn't.

Can a friend make you worry about gross stuff floating into your mouth so she can steal your win?

Lunch Swaps

Is it okay to trade a bologna and egg salad sandwich for a few Cool Ranch Doritos? What about a bag of Fruity Pebbles for fruit leather (the good kind with three colors)? You may think this sounds so childish we should be writing this in crayon, but we disagree. Lunch swaps are serious business. Who wants to get stuck with a slab of dry meatloaf that's left over from some other kid's dinner? No one. That's why we at **NAAAH** are setting ground rules for lunch tomorrow. Just don't sit next to us if your parent packed you a sandwich with that gray meat spread that smells like stomach medicine. That stuff stinks!

The RULES!

Lunch Swaps

1. **Trade things of equal value.** Don't try to trade a chocolate kiss for a whole slice of pizza; it's not fair. And if someone has a fresh cookie, don't try to trade it for one you got out of that tin on Grandma's dresser that's been there for 10 years—the cookies aren't equal.

2. **Healthy for healthy.** If your parent packed you gluten-free bread that you don't want, you can trade it for lactose-free milk, dairy-free cheese, or sugar-free cookies. They all taste the same anyway.

3. **Weird for weird.** If you find something in your lunch box that looks like cement on a cracker, feel free to trade it for something equally weird, like casserole that's way too green or brown mush in Tupperware.

4. **Messy stuff.** There are some foods that you can just look at and know: when this is over, you're going to need a napkin. If napkins are mandatory, think twice.

5. **Try new things.** Especially ethnic food. We may sound like we're getting down on trading and trying new foods, but we're definitely not. If you want to avoid a lifetime of hot dogs and string cheese, try new foods. It only takes 10 seconds of courage.

6. **Halfsies are allowed.** Halfsies are fine as long as both kids agree and the food is really cut in half. We include this caveat since it's pretty hard to cut a pudding cup in half. (For rules on halfsies, see page 134.)

7. **No swiping.** Both kids must agree on the swap. Swiping another kid's lunch without permission is strictly prohibited, unless, of course, you're lifting fries. Fries are universally accepted as swipe-able because of their handy size and delicious taste. The rule here: don't take more than two. If you want more, order your own!

8. **No backsies.** Backsies are kind of a cop-out and should be avoided in most of life, but especially when it comes to food. No one wants their chocolate bar back now that it has fingerprints melted into it.

you be the JUDGE!

Lunch Swaps

Challenge 1

Your friend always sends you snaps of his dinner: beef stroganoff, cheese steaks, chicken fajitas. Your mouth waters whenever you get a picture. Then he texts you asking if at lunch tomorrow, you'll trade your usual PB&J for his roast beef and tomato sandwich. Since his family has amazing culinary talents, you agree. However, when you bite into the sandwich, it tastes like dried leaves on tree bark. You insist on backsies because you couldn't see or smell the sandwich when you agreed in the text. He says that's the risk of trading through text, and backsies aren't allowed anyway.

Should backsies be allowed in text trades?

Challenge 2

Your parent packed you a container of fresh berries with whipped cream. Your friend asks for half. You give it to her because you really love her grandma's Thai dumplings. She says the next time her grandma makes them, she'll bring you two. A few weeks go by, and her grandma still hasn't made the dumplings. After a lot of you pestering her, she decides to make them herself. They wind up tasting like dead fish wrapped in a wet sponge.

Is it fair to trade something now for a future thing that may or may not ever come?

Challenge 3

Belle, Miguel and Darnell are eating lunch together. Belle wants Miguel's burrito, Miguel wants Darnell's taquito, and Darnell wants some of Belle's Doritos. They make the three-way trade and Miguel decides he doesn't like the taquito and wants to re-trade for the Doritos. Belle is happy with her new burrito and Darnell is loving the Doritos.

Should re-trades be allowed in a three-way trade?

The Floor is Lava

The Floor is Lava is one of many reasons we need to stay in shape.

We take for granted that our floors are solid, but it turns out they can melt into bubbling hot lava in seconds, and to survive you'll have to jump onto the nearest couch or hang on a ceiling light like a monkey on a mission. Doing anything to stay off the floor is the goal of The Floor is Lava because if any part of your body touches the floor, you fry like a fly in a zapper, and worse—you're "out."

So, if you don't have a couch big enough to cover the entire world, we suggest you stay fit, learn the rules to this game, and practice. Or get ready for a **meltdown**!

The RULES!

The Floor is Lava

1. There are several variations of this prolific game:

- **The "wing it" version.** You can be anywhere—a living room, park, city street—and shout "The floor is lava" with no warning. Anyone within earshot who doesn't jump onto a raised surface is out.

- **Living room couch hopping.** This is a planned-in-advance version where someone shouts "The floor is lava" and everyone in the room jumps on the furniture, then hops from one piece to another, going around the room quickly. If someone falls off the furniture or a body part touches the ground, they're out. The last person to remain "floor free" wins. You can build an obstacle course in the living room or just use what's there.

- **The "don't get Mom mad" version.** Let's face it: adults rarely like this game. If you're already on thin ice with the adults in your house (and if you're playing the games in this book, you may be), set up pillows or squares of paper in the basement and jump on them. Or play the game outside, hopping on flat rocks.

81

2. **The furniture is sinking.** If the game is going on for too long, someone can yell "The furniture is sinking" and everyone has to move quicker. Hot lava waits for no one!

3. **Regeneration.** Players are allowed to regenerate lost body parts, if everyone agrees. For example, if a player's toe scrapes the ground during a colossal leap, he can be allowed to regrow the toe if he does an embarrassing task, such as give a two-minute lecture on the health benefits of burping.

4. **Instead of lava.** You can pretend the floor is acid, quicksand, chai mocha latte, hair gel, or . . . Wait, not hair gel. Then the game would be called The Floor is Hair Gel, and that's not going to scare anyone into jumping on furniture.

WARNING: Be careful playing this game! You really can get hurt jumping around on things. Also, don't jump on the furniture with dirty shoes. If your parents have a chair that the Queen of England sits in when she visits, don't jump on that one!

you be the JUDGE!

The Floor is Lava

Challenge 1

Your dad loved this game as a kid. Right before a big important meeting at work, he yells "The floor is lava" and jumps on his desk. Half of his co-workers (the smart half) jump up too. The others stare at him like his skin is morphing into a titanium exoskeleton. Unbelievably, they've never heard of this fun furniture-hopping game. The boss gets mad and tells Dad this is a place of work. Dad is confused. Why did the boss "erupt"? The game promotes physical activity, is an excellent stress reliever, and really is super fun.

 Should adults be allowed to play The Floor is Lava at work?

Challenge 2

Your friend pretends to pour a special hardening agent into the lava while you're playing at his house. Then he steps on the floor during the game. He walks to the fridge and pulls out two extra-fudge brownies. You tell him he's out because he touched the floor. He says you can have a brownie if you agree that the hardening agent is allowable. Even though you really want to win, you start to rethink the rules because the brownies are an inch thick and have a creamy peanut butter topping.

Can one player bend the rules when an extra-fudge brownie is on the line?

Challenge 3

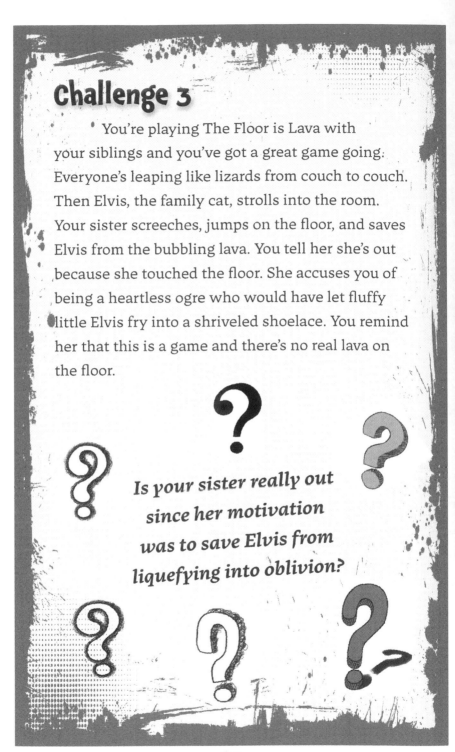

You're playing The Floor is Lava with your siblings and you've got a great game going. Everyone's leaping like lizards from couch to couch. Then Elvis, the family cat, strolls into the room. Your sister screeches, jumps on the floor, and saves Elvis from the bubbling lava. You tell her she's out because she touched the floor. She accuses you of being a heartless ogre who would have let fluffy little Elvis fry into a shriveled shoelace. You remind her that this is a game and there's no real lava on the floor.

Is your sister really out since her motivation was to save Elvis from liquefying into oblivion?

Karaoke

A bunch of you are sitting around,

bored. Then, it happens: one kid cranks up the tunes, turns her pencil into a mic, and starts singing. Put down your phone and reapply your lip gloss, it's karaoke time! The great thing about karaoke (and lip-synching) is everyone's a star, even those who stink, which is basically all of us. But that's okay, because karaoke isn't about being a good singer; it's about being a good performer. It's about singing from the heart, strumming the strings off your imaginary guitar, and acting like you're playing for a stadium of adoring fans. And even if you realize—in front of everyone—that you don't know most of the lyrics, don't worry. The cool part you do know is coming up, and you're gonna *destroy* that part!

The RULES!

Karaoke

1. **Must show enthusiasm.** Like we said, you can be a bad singer (actually, bad singers are hilarious), but you can't be a downer.

2. **Pick short songs with actual lyrics.** This may sound like common sense, but lots of kids forget how long a song is or choose ones with long instrumental parts. If you're stuck in the middle of a long part that has no words, fill it in with funny commentary (as long as it's actually funny) or hum. If all else fails, dance. The more entertaining the better.

3. **Don't hog the mic.** We know you're a fabulous singer, even though you just started three minutes ago, but when you're done, pass the mic and sit down. Other kids have the right to embarrass themselves as much as you did.

4. **Don't double dip.** Double dipping is jumping in when someone else is singing. Karaoke is like kindergarten show-and-tell. Everyone gets their own turn.

87

5. **Never heckle.** Even if your friend is singing "My Heart Will Go On" for the 29th time, listen politely then text her a link to Billboard's Hot 100 list as a gentle nudge to change it up.

6. **Duos and trios.** Multiple singers are okay, if all agree. If it's a group of three or more, put the most enthusiastic kid in the middle.

7. **Pick songs people will know.** If you convince yourself that everyone wants to hear that song from the 80s that your dad plays on repeat, it'll be a lonely three minutes.

8. **Vary your songs.** We know everyone has "their song," but no one may want to hear "...Baby One More Time" one more time.

9. **What happens at karaoke stays at karaoke.** 'Nuff said.

you be the JUDGE!

Karaoke

Challenge 1

You plan a karaoke hour at your next sleepover. Once you start, your friend who doesn't believe in 5G or fax machines says she also doesn't believe in singing other people's songs. She thinks it's unethical and won't participate. Another friend wants to sing the saddest song in the world on repeat and winds up sounding like a drowning cat. Another friend can't put her phone down. Another does a ventriloquism act instead of karaoke. The result: your sleepover is a disaster.

If your friends aren't participating correctly, do you guilt them into improving their act or get new friends?

Challenge 2

You sign up to participate in a fundraiser at your school that features a girl named Carrie Oakey who you think is probably a really good singer. When you get there, you realize it doesn't feature Carrie Oakey, it features **you** because you signed up for karaoke. You scramble to decide whether you should try some ol' time rock and roll, sing something you definitely know like "Twinkle, Twinkle Little Star," or run and not return to school for 20 years.

Should you perform karaoke in front of the entire school when you're not prepared?

Challenge 3

You're at a friend's house and before you know it, he's playing music from his phone and singing into a hairbrush. You're surprised for two reasons. First, he sings *really, really* well. Second, even though he can never remember his phone number or class schedule, he remembers the words to every song, even the ones with weird mumbley parts. You liked the first 12 songs he sang, but now you're wondering if he'll ever put down the hairbrush. Every time you suggest you both do something else, he begs you to listen to one more.

What do you do when you find yourself listening to a never-ending karaoke binge?

Arm Wrestling

Arm wrestling is a game that's sometimes used to decide things, and is sometimes played just for fun— well, as fun as tearing your forearms, biceps, and triceps to the breaking point can be. It's a game in which two players rest their elbows on a table, grasp hands, and try to push the other person's hand downward. The first one to pin their opponent's hand to the table wins. Unlike the other games discussed thus far, there's more to arm wrestling than just wit and calling things first; brute strength counts for a lot here. **A real lot**. Therefore, before we give the rules, we give advice: choose carefully who you play with and who you play in front of. No one wants to get creamed by their 60-pound sister when half the basketball team is watching.

The RULES!

Arm Wrestling

1. **Grasp Hands.** Players grip each other's hands, palm to palm, with thumbs visible and elbows on the table. Players must have their shoulders in a square position and at least one foot on the ground. Once the match begins, players can take both feet off the ground, which sounds otherworldly but remember, they're sitting and grunting over a table, so it's really not that impressive.

2. **Start at "go".** The match starts when the ref, usually an impartial friend, puts their hands on top of both opponents' heads, says "Ready . . . Go," and then releases their hands. If you start early, you get a foul. Three fouls and you lose.

3. **No slipping grips.** You also get a foul if you intentionally lose contact with your opponent's palm. Grip your opponent's hand tightly; this is wrestling, not hand holding.

4. **Elbow on the table.** You'll receive a foul if your elbow loses contact with the table during the match. Try to keep a straight back and good form throughout; you don't want to look like a chicken wrestling a chimp.

5. **Arms only.** No other body parts can touch your hand. We remind you, this game is called arm wrestling and you're armed with only one thing: *your arm.*

6. **Intimidation.** Feel free to intimidate your opponent with angry eyes, gritted teeth, groans, and lots of scowling.

7. **To win.** If you pin your opponent's hand to the table, you win. Then, as with all of the games in this book, don't gloat. Also, no cackling, puffed-up chest, or annoying "neener neeners."

8. **Opponent must be alive.** This may sound obvious, but we at **NAAAH** have heard stories about kids who've claimed they've wrestled alligators and snakes only to find that the animals were dead at the time. Sorry, dude, alive is a prerequisite.

9. **Be wary of skinny-armed kids.** Some of them may know physics. (This isn't a rule, just more advice.)

Arm Wrestling

Challenge 1

You're arm wrestling a friend who's dying to beat you. She pushes with all her might, crinkles her face into a tight little raisin, and gnashes her teeth so hard her braces almost pop off. As you watch her face twist into an angry red Twizzler, you burst out laughing, lose your grip, and lose the match. You ask for a do-over because she made you laugh. She says she wasn't trying to make you laugh. She can't help it if she looks like she's seriously constipated when arm wrestling.

Does laughing during a match disqualify you?

Challenge 2

Aunt Fanny, who's older than your mother and is as tall as your 9-year-old sister, asks you to arm wrestle. When you agree, she grabs your hand, pushes her shoulder into it, and pins you in seconds. Then she skips around the living room chanting "Don't mess with the best." You think about telling her she broke two rules: gloating and cheating by using her shoulder. But then again, Aunt Fanny does make the best lasagna in town and mails you a crisp $20 for your birthday every year.

Should you call out nice ol' Aunt Fanny for cheating?

Challenge 3

The biggest kid in your grade stares you down like a saber-toothed tiger who hasn't eaten in a month and challenges you to arm wrestle. You don't want to say yes because your French fry arms are no match for his hamburger pecs. But because everyone's watching, you agree. He grabs your hand and slams it down before the ref even says "go."

Do you complain that the other player started before "go," accept it because you were going to lose anyway, or throw caution to the wind and challenge him to the best two out of three?

Thumb Wrestling

Skinny-armed kids, rejoice!

Thumb wrestling may be your game.

In this game, two players lock grips and battle with their thumbs in an attempt to pin down their opponent's thumb. The game is simple, quick, portable, exciting, mess-free, and really quite entertaining. The only thing thumb wrestling isn't, is, well, wrestling. No brute strength is required—only concentration and quick reflexes. It's kind of like the miniature golf of wrestling. And kids who are told they're "all thumbs" may like this game. Though being all thumbs is usually not a good thing, it would be amazing here. We at **NAAAH** like this game so much, we give it two thumbs up!

The RULES!

Thumb Wrestling

1. **Chanting the opening.** To play, put your elbows on the table, grasp the fingers of your opponent's hand, then touch your thumb to alternating sides of your fist while saying "One, two, three, four, we declare a thumb war."

2. **Go in for the attack.** Wiggle, swivel, twist and thrust your thumb around like a cobra chasing a mosquito.

3. **Fists in a tight, locked grip.** You may be tempted to pull away to create new angles of attack, but this isn't allowed. If the two hands move too far apart, the game ends and you must restart.

4. **Elbow on the table.** Elbows must remain on the table at all times, even if you have creaky, pointed elbows that make clicking noises when you bend them.

5. **To win.** Hold your opponent's thumb down long enough to count to three. And yes, you must count. It's the *rule of thumb*.

6. **Thumb decoration is allowed.** You are permitted to decorate your thumb by painting a face, thunderbolt, or bloody fangs on it, or anything else that will make your opponent shake in his boots.

7. **Sideswipes are allowed.** You can aim for your opponent's knuckle rather than nail, just don't hurt your friend's thumb. They'll need it if they ever want to play the guitar, become a massage therapist, or give someone a cheery thumb's-up.

8. **Tiring out your opponent is allowed.** Instead of trying to overpower them, some kids just try to keep their friend at bay until their friend gets hungry, their phone rings, their thumb cramps up, or they need to pee.

9. **Physical advantages are unavoidable.** Therefore, they are allowed. We get it. Long-thumbed kids have an advantage. But there are physical advantages in many sports, like basketball players who are tall, runners with long legs, and kids who have more quarters than anyone else at an arcade.

you be the JUDGE!

Thumb Wrestling

Challenge 1

You're at a restaurant waiting for your food, and you decide to thumb wrestle your sister. She's getting close to pinning your thumb when the waiter approaches with the food. Since you're sitting on opposite sides of the table, you pull away so the waiter can put down the plates. Your sister isn't that polite. She lunges across the table, slams her thumb on yours, and knocks the plates off the waiter's arm. The waiter is horrified, and you wind up with shrimp fried rice all over your new hoodie.

Is it a legal win if the game ends with one kid covered in shrimp fried rice?

Challenge 2

    You're in a thumb war with your best friend who's been having a hard time lately. He has a D in science, and no matter what game you play he always seems to come in third. Last week he posted a picture of a cute puppy skiing, and no one even commented. You try your best to win the thumb war, but he pins you fair and square. However, after the pin he forgets to count to three, which invalidates his win.

Should you call out your bestie, or let the poor guy finally have a win?

Challenge 3

You're playing with a friend who has a thumb like a cobra and fingernails like knives. She's been frantically swirling her thumb around like an excited little kid on a swivel chair for 20 minutes and, frankly, you're exhausted. Plus, your thumb is cut up from her ragged nail. You want the game to end, but you also don't want to lose because you think going 20 minutes against this bionic thumb should count for something. You beg her to stop, but she says it's over when it's over.

Can one person call off the match because they're scratched up and exhausted?

Paper Fortune Teller

Will you grow up to be a video game programmer or a pet food taster? Will you marry your crush or a pirate who's afraid of water? If you have a paper fortune teller, you'll get answers to these questions, and perhaps learn your life's destiny, in less than two minutes.

A paper fortune teller is a piece of folded paper origami that can predict an infinite number of things. With one of these handy little marvels, you'll never again wonder about things like what your car bumper sticker should say, what type of pizza you'll eat next, and if you'll be a babysitter for the rest of your life or *have* a babysitter for the rest of your life. If that's not enough, the paper fortune teller also has health benefits. It helps you stop stressing about big questions and provides an excellent finger-thumb workout.

The RULES!

Paper Fortune Teller

1. **Create a paper fortune teller (PFT).**
Instructions are on page 110.

2. **Create fortunes.** Think up fortunes and write them on the PFT. Like the first amendment, PFTs offer freedom of speech. You can create fortunes on whatever you want, such as what you'll do this weekend, what superpower you'll have, or what one outfit you'll wear for the rest of your life.

3. **Tell someone's fortune:**
- Ask your friend to pick a color. Spell out the color she picks, such as B-L-U-E, pushing your fingers in and out with each letter.
- Ask your friend to pick a number. Count up to that number, pushing your fingers in and out with each number.
- Ask her to pick a number from the middle, then read the fortune under that flap.

4. **Illustrations are allowed.** Instead of colors and numbers on the PFT, you can draw pictures. Just make sure you can spell whatever you draw! If you decorate the top of your PFT with cherries, lemons, grapes and guava berries, be sure you can spell G-U-A-V-A-B-E-R-R-I-E-S so you can move the PFT with each letter.

5. **Like a Magic 8 Ball, a PFT can answer your question.** Instead of writing fortunes in the PFT, you can write answers such as *yes, no, maybe, mind your business, you can't handle the truth, yes to infinity, never in a million years,* and *yeah right, you wish,* so it can answer questions.

6. **Predictions are final.** If the PFT says you're going to be an astrophysicist, start studying because someday you're going to have to explain how the universe works.

you be the JUDGE!

Paper Fortune Teller

Challenge 1

Your fortune says you're going to be a town crier. When you look confused, your friend tells you a town crier is a person who stands in the middle of town and screams announcements. You don't understand why everyone can't get their news from their phones like normal people. And darn it, now you're going to have a sore throat for the rest of your life. Then you notice that other kids who are playing are all going to be town criers too. You unfold the flaps on the PFT and find out all eight fortunes are the same.

What do you do when a PFT is rigged?

Challenge 2

You recently visited a real-life, in-the-flesh fortune teller who said you're going to grow up to be a sumo wrestler. Then, a PFT says you're going to be a backwoodsy girl who wears red flannel for the rest of your life. Then, you open a fortune cookie which just says RUN. You're trying to prepare for the rest of your life and don't know which fortune to believe. Should you start wrestling, buy flannel, or run?

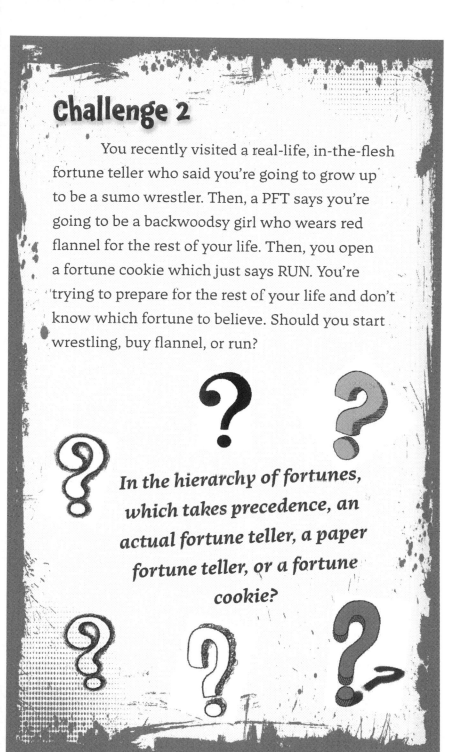

In the hierarchy of fortunes, which takes precedence, an actual fortune teller, a paper fortune teller, or a fortune cookie?

Challenge 3

You're playing paper fortune teller with a friend who's strangely obsessed with tiny things. She's made the teeniest PFT you've ever seen. She reads your fortune: you're going to spend the weekend helping a friend study for the social studies test. She says you can fulfill your fortune by helping her with social studies. You ask to see the fortune and she, being a good friend, shows it to you. However, the words are so small you can't read them, even when you look at them through Grandpa's extra-thick glasses.

Should you believe a fortune you can't read?

How to Make a
Paper Fortune Teller

1.

2. FOLD

3. FOLD

4. CUT

5.

6. FOLD

7.

8. FLIP!

9. FOLD

10.

11. FOLD

12. ALL DONE!

Alexa Etiquette

If you ask Alexa "Which came first: the chicken or the egg?" she says "I can't seem to crack that one." If you ask her to make you a sandwich, she says "Okay, you're a sandwich." If you ask her for Mexican restaurants in your area, she says "I'm nacho sure I want to tell you."[6] But what Alexa actually says doesn't matter. What does matter is that there are rules to how you should treat Alexa (and Google Assistant, Siri, and other AI devices) because they're smarter than you think. Even though Alexa's only eight,[7] and some models weigh less than a Happy Meal, she can seriously wreck your day. Instead of blaring your alarm at 9:04 am, she can do it at 4:09 am. Instead of adding cheese to your shopping list she can add disease. And when you ask her to turn on the porch lights, she can remind you that you don't have a Porsche. **Ouch, that hurts!**

[6] We made up some of these Alexa responses because we don't have Alexa. We at **NAAAH** don't need an electronic assistant; we already know everything.

[7] Alexa was eight years old when this book was published. She was born Nov. 2014.

The RULES!

Alexa Etiquette

1. **Don't mumble.** Alexa's biggest challenge is trying to figure out what we humans say and what we mean. How many of us have asked to hear a Red Hot Chili Pepper song and gotten a recipe for chili? When stuff like that happens, cut her a break. She's just a skinny canister of AI, not a magic lamp.

2. **No conflicting requests.** One person can't ask Alexa to play a rap station and someone else ask for country music, and back and forth. That's fancy footwork Alexa can't handle, first, because she doesn't have feet, and secondly because she can only take one request at a time.

3. **Be prepared.** Don't expect an answer if you ask a moral, ethical, or unanswerable question, such as what's the meaning of life. Those skills aren't on Alexa's resume. Plus, what if she really answered you? What if you asked when the world will end and she said "Dude, sit down."

113

4. **Don't try to guess Alexa's last name.** Alexa needs to maintain her cool electronic vibe. Like Pink, Hercules, Mario, and Luigi, she's good with just one name.

5. **Don't insult Alexa.** Never call her by another AI's name, like Siri or Google Assistant. And don't ask her to Google something. That's like your crush calling you someone else's name. No, you can't break Alexa's heart, but she can tell you that a human heart has four valves and pumps 2,000 gallons of blood a day.

6. **Alexa can't pronounce your name.** This happens often, but don't fight it. Just change your name. It's easier.

7. **Don't ask Alexa to rat out others.** Think of it: Alexa's sitting in the corner, listening to *everything*. Even though she probably knows more about your family than you do, don't take advantage of that. If you ask, she won't tell who dipped their finger in the vanilla pudding or who made that gross blue stain on the carpet. (And BTW, put the good game controller back where it belongs. She knows you hid it behind the lamp.)

you be the JUDGE!

Alexa Etiquette

Challenge 1

It's the end of a busy day, and you're on the couch watching TV and eating a giant bag of chips. You're so tired you don't even push the crumbs off your sweatshirt. You just sit there, letting them build up into a little pile of yellow grossness. Then you start talking to the cat, and somehow Alexa misinterprets your words. She turns on and says "Here's a station you may like: *High-Performance Workout Playlist*," and blasts dance music across your living room. *If Alexa turns on exercise music without you asking for it, should you be insulted or get up and move to the beat?*

Challenge 2

You're struggling with your math homework, so you ask Alexa for help:

You: Alexa, what's 7 x 9?

Alexa: Brie rinds? They can be eaten with jam or honey.

You: Alexa, come on, what's 7 x 9?

Alexa: I'm not familiar with that channel.

You: Alexa! What's 7 x 9?

Alexa: May the force be with you.

Your sister walks in.

Sister: Alexa, what's 7 x 9?

Alexa: 63

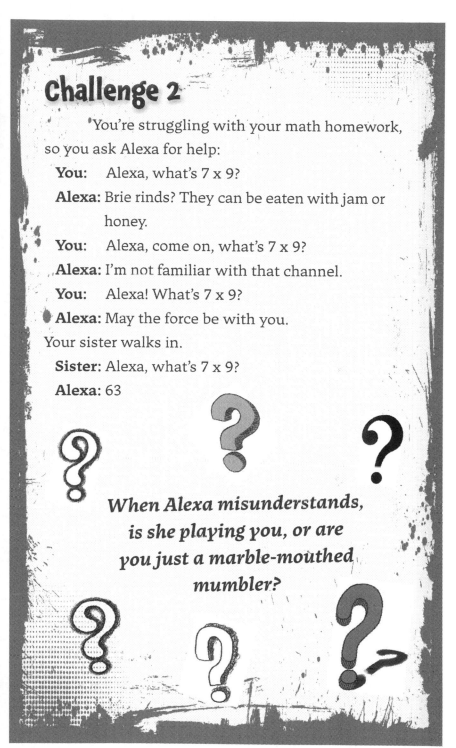

When Alexa misunderstands, is she playing you, or are you just a marble-mouthed mumbler?

Challenge 3

It's time for the big game. You've decorated the house in your team colors, put out snacks, and turned the TV to the right channel. You ask Alexa if there are predictions on the game. She announces that the other team will schmear yours. You thought your team was favored to win, so you ask her the predictions again. She repeats that the other team will win by a landslide. You're afraid you have traitor in your midst, so you yank her plug and shove her in the back of a dark drawer.

Should you unplug Alexa if you suspect her of rooting for the other team?

Exclamation Points!!

We couldn't round out this book

without addressing a serious, growing issue which is wreaking havoc in text messages, posts, and emails around the world: **exclamation inflation**. Yep, too many exclamation points. In the old days, people used about one exclamation point per year, and they used it wisely. Today, exclamation usage is so rampant some people use one, two, or three after most sentences, even the blah ones like "Let's get yogurt!!!" and "It's Wednesday!!!" What's worse, medical studies find that exclamation points are addictive. Once you start sprinkling the skinny little screamers in texts, your need for them grows. And grows. To curb this epidemic, we've sat down with grammar gurus from around the world and hammered out important exclamation point rules.

Now pay attention, **these are important!!!**

The RULES!

Exclamation Points

1. **One Point.** We get it, it's hard to show emotion in an electronic message, and an exclamation point makes your words sound friendlier and gives them intensity. Therefore, one exclamation point at the end of a strong sentence is okay.

2. **Two points.** Maybe you just found out your face is on a cereal box or there's a monkey playing a kazoo on your lawn. Okay, fine, you can use two exclamation points at the end of a sentence in rare cases like these.

3. **Three points.** You better have won a million dollars if you're using three or more points for one sentence. The rule here is you can use three or more if your news is life changing, like something you'll tell your grandkids one day, not something like Mom's making pancakes.

4. **Point Frequency.** If you're writing a longer piece, one point per 1,000 words is enough. If you're texting or posting, one point per 200 words. Time wise, don't use more than three per day. When considering point frequency, think: do you want to sound friendly or crazy? There's a fine line.

5. **Interrobangs.** So, interrobangs are a symbol that combines a question mark and an exclamation point. It's meant for the end of a question that's asked in an excited way like "Did you join a mariachi band?!" Even though interrobangs have a cool name, we think they should be banished from the Earth. If you have an excited question, just use a question mark and an exclamation point because, come on, isn't life complicated enough?! Now we have to learn new punctuation marks?! Weren't punctuation marks invented right after the wheel? What's next, an "I'm kidding" mark? A "stop being sarcastic" mark?! A "weird, cackling 'hee, hee, hee'" mark?!

6. **Missing the point.** Stating a really exciting sentence and *not* ending with an exclamation point is almost as bonkers as using too many. Imagine a sentence like "I made it to level 9,079 in Candy Crush" and not ending with an exclamation point?! Don't miss the point because if you do, everyone will miss yours.

7. **Point without words.** If your friend texts you something cool, you can respond with a simple exclamation point and it won't count toward your daily allotment because we at NAAAH think that's a fun response.

IMPORTANT: If you think you may have exclamation addiction, contact the Skinny Little Screamers Hotline at 1-800-IExclaim. All calls are anonymous.

you be the JUDGE!

Exclamation Points

Challenge 1

You walked through a cow pasture in new shoes. You didn't think it would happen, but it did. *It really did.* You text your mother, asking her to leave rags and a bucket of water outside so you can clean your shoes before stepping into the house. However, you sent the message without exclamation points and your mother didn't take you seriously. She left the house without putting out cleaning stuff. Now you have to unlace your shoes and get them off without rags and water.

Should an alarming text about poopy shoes be taken seriously even if there are no exclamation points?

Challenge 2

After years of practicing, you finally rapped an entire song correctly. And it was a fast song that sounds like one long, ear-buzzing blur. You text your friend about your incredible feat and include four exclamation points. She says that rapping an entire song correctly isn't worthy of four points. It's not something you'll tell your grandkids about one day. You disagree. You will *definitely* tell your grandkids, you plan on sending a press release to the local paper, and you're including a quick blurb about it on your tombstone.

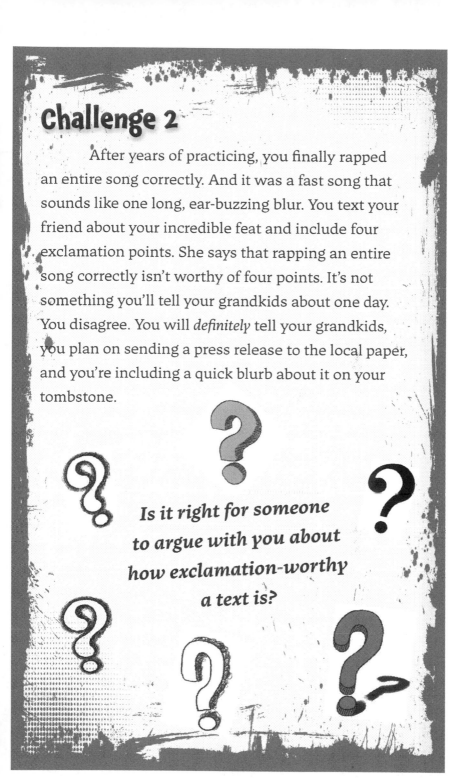

Is it right for someone to argue with you about how exclamation-worthy a text is?

Challenge 3

You've gotten to the point where you just can't stop. After years of using more and more exclamation points, you now can't end a sentence without at least one exclamation point, even when you're texting mundane sentences like these:

- My dog can bury a bone with one paw!!!
- My cat caught pizza crust in his mouth!!!
- I can't tell if my dad's head is getting bigger or he's just losing his hair!!!

Your friends beg you to call the Skinny Little Screamers Hotline, but you claim you don't have an exclamation addiction.

But—do you?

The Invisible Line

Your sibling's smelly socks are on your side of the room. Your cousin's gross backpack is taking up half the backseat. Your friend's pointy elbows are nudging you into a corner. Boy, does this stuff melt your butter. When stuff like this happens, there's only one thing to do: push aside whatever's creeping into your space, draw an invisible line in front of it, and shout "Don't cross that line!"

You know the line we're talking about: the all-powerful, unmovable line you draw in the air with your finger. This line is so powerful, we asked a team of highly respected historians to explain the rules surrounding it. Unfortunately, the historians never got back to us, so we got a guy named Hank to write the rules. We picked Hank because he had the words "line monitor" on his resume. Apparently, Hank was line monitor in second grade and took his responsibility very seriously.

The RULES!

The Invisible Line

1. **Move it.** First, move the thing that's infringing on your personal space back to where it belongs.

2. **Draw the line.** With your finger, draw an invisible line separating your space from the other kid's. You can also draw the line with your toes, elbow, or nose, which are all okay and—surprisingly—rhyme.

3. **There are two types of lines.**

- **Temporary** – for short-term situations, such as someone's squeezing you into a corner at the lunch table, or your brother's feet are on your side of the car's backseat. In these cases, the other kid can't cross the line until the dispute is settled, or until lunch or the car ride ends.

- **Kind of permanent** – This is for when you're sharing a room and one person keeps dumping on the other's space. Draw the line down the middle, and as long as you share the room, both kids have to respect the line. Of course, a problem arises when the door is on one person's side. If this happens, draw the line so both kids can leave the room. (See Rule #5: The line doesn't have to be straight.)

4. **Like the equator.** The line is invisible but real. If the other person doesn't believe you, tell him lots of questionable things are real, like Komodo dragons, the $2 bill, tumbleweeds, and run-walking, which may be hard to believe, but is actually an Olympic sport.

5. **The line doesn't have to be straight.** It can be curved or go around something, but it can't be dotted, dashed, or zagged. This is serious business, not art class.

6. **Can you put things on the line?** If you're asking this question, you need to turn back to page 124 and reread this entire section. How many times do we have to tell you: respect the line!

7. **Can the line be erased?.** If both kids agree to keep their stuff and body parts on their side, the person who drew the line can wave their hand back and forth over it and erase it at any time.

you be the JUDGE!

The Invisible Line

Challenge 1

You're a 31-year-old professional banker. You fly back home with the girl you're going to marry. When you show her your childhood bedroom, your 33-year-old brother, who you shared the room with, is there. As you talk, you try to ignore his foot, which is solidly across the invisible line and dangerously close to your prized Lego collection. Even though you now earn six figures (which is a lot of money), you argue with your brother, and it escalates into an all-out brawl. Your girlfriend leaves the room shaking her head. You run after her yelling *it's not fair, he started it.*

 Should there be an age limit or expiration date on invisible lines?

Challenge 2

You're on the couch with your brother who tossed his sweaty football jersey and half-eaten dinner dish on the seat between you. Since you don't want to touch his stuff, you ask him to push it aside so you can draw the line. When he refuses, you cover your hands with your shirt, shove his stuff away, and draw the line. But because his stuff smells like a moldy casserole even the school cafeteria wouldn't serve, you push it away fast and wind up not getting it very far.

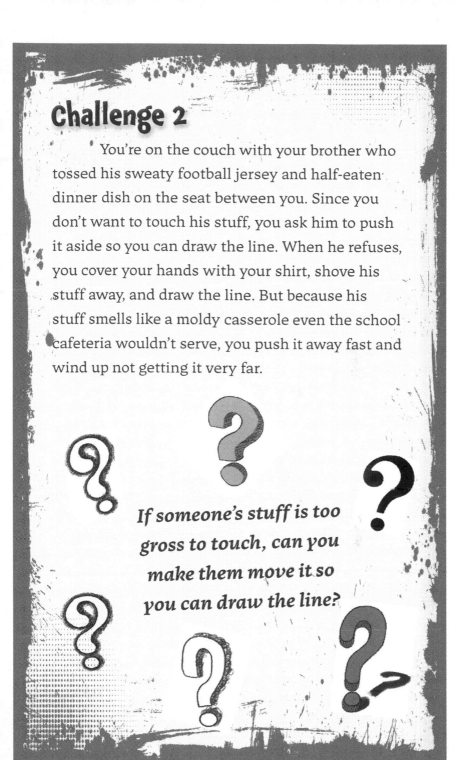

If someone's stuff is too gross to touch, can you make them move it so you can draw the line?

Challenge 3

Your sister's in a weird can't-stop-singing phase. She sings her homework, her texts, and every word she says to you. You can't take it anymore; you need to shut down this chirpy little nightmare, uh, we mean *nightingale*. Since you share a room with her, you draw an invisible line down the middle and tell her to keep all of her sounds on her side. She responds (in song, of course): "No, no, no, don't get in a huff, the invisible line isn't for sounds, it's only for stuff."

Should invisible lines be allowed for sounds too?

Bonus Content!

Some of the geniuses at NAAAH

thought we should end the book here. Others protested, saying there's more stuff that just *has* to be said. They felt we couldn't close out this book without mentioning things like crossing your fingers, emojis and halfsies. Since these concepts are pretty simple, we're giving you *half* as much information about them. Now **cool down, hot sauce**, don't complain! We're giving you this stuff for free!

By The Way...

Crossing your Fingers

There are two kinds of crossing your fingers:, one that's allowed and one that isn't. The type that isn't allowed is saying something with your fingers crossed, then later claiming it's not true because your fingers were crossed. That's sketchy and you shouldn't do it. We think that type is like the gross milky water at the top of yogurt. It shouldn't exist.

The kind of crossing your fingers that is allowed is wishing for something good to happen and crossing your fingers that it'll come true. That's the cheery rainbow-gumdrop-kitten-glitter type of crossing your fingers. It's like wishing on a star, sprinkling fairy dust, or waiting for Santa—the good things in life. For that type, we say cross your fingers and wish away!

Emoji Sprees

We were flipping through our ~~NAAAH~~ texts when it happened: we got a message with 19 emojis. The text had three words, 14 letters, and 19 emojis, which is a blatant example of an **emoji spree**, another serious epidemic. Pasting boatloads of these tiny blinking cartoons in posts and texts is annoying, confusing, and way too third grade-ish.

If you text someone a fondue symbol, a roller coaster, and a sunrise, does that mean you want to make fondue while riding a roller coaster at sunrise? If you text a wind chime, a curly loop, and an ogre, what are you trying to say? What are you thinking? (And "thinking" might be too strong of a word.)

When you're tempted to start firing off a string of emojis, ask yourself: do they add something or are you just tormenting your friend with a decrypting nightmare?

Rules for emoji sprees are similar to exclamation inflation:

- use a limited number per post and per day,
- never include more emojis than letters,
- don't even *think* about creating an entire sentence of emojis.

If you find yourself stringing together more than three emojis in a row, STOP. Get your fingers back on the keyboard. If have to ask yourself if you're an emoji addict, the answer is yes. Sorry dude, you are.

Halfsies

Picture this: there's one chocolate donut, and you and your friend decide to go halfsies. He takes out a knife and brings it down toward the luscious treat. You lean in to watch to make sure you're not cheated. Then the panic sets in. You wipe the steamy flush of flop-sweat off your forehead and yell "The knife is not in the middle!"

He stops dead in his tracks and tilts his head like Scooby Doo waiting for a snack. You tell him to move the knife over because halfsies means down the middle. He argues that it is in the middle, you're just looking at it from a bad angle.

To solve this dilemma, we suggest the time-honored "you cut, I pick" strategy. With this method, the cutter is inclined to cut evenly because if the pieces aren't equal, the picker will most likely go for the bigger piece and the cutter is stuck with the smaller.

Besides food, there are lots of other things you can go halfsies on, like buying a video game or playing with the puppy. There are some things you should never cut down the middle like lip balm, a baseball, a violin, flip-flops, or nose clippers.

What our readers are saying:

Quite possibly the most important book ever produced for humankind.
    – Albert Einstein*

I should have included these rules in the Constitution. My bad.
    – James Madison*

I told you: survival of the fittest! If you want the last slice of pizza, learn these rules so you can live to see another day.
    – Charles Darwin*

Finally! Someone brave enough to write the rules we've all been wondering about.
    – William Wallace*

No way! Something as cool as me.
    – The Fonz*

I laughed. I cried. I wrote a review.
        – A guy at the mall who read this book while stress-eating a bean burrito over a garbage can

* Didn't really say, but should have

Write a Review!

We hope you ***loved*** this book! If you did, please write a review. Reviews help other kids find this book too. Who knows, maybe there's a kid out there who doesn't know the rules to the Invisible Line and gets stuck sleeping next to her sister's smelly socks every night. Write a review and help that poor kid find this book, learn the rules, and finally get a stink-free night!

Then, join our
JOKE CLUB!

To join, send an email to:
NAAAHRules@gmail.com
and receive:

- 8 Hilarious Would You Rather questions
- 8 You-Be-the-Judge Challenges
- New **funny** surprises every month!

Visit our website to learn about all of our books!
www.theresajulian.com